LEADERS LIKE US
DALIP SINGH SAUND

BY KAREN SU
ILLUSTRATED BY ARLO LI

Rourke

ROURKE'S SCHOOL to HOME CONNECTIONS
BEFORE AND DURING READING ACTIVITIES

Before Reading: *Building Background Knowledge and Vocabulary*

Building background knowledge can help children process new information and build upon what they already know. Before reading a book, it is important to tap into what children already know about the topic. This will help them develop their vocabulary and increase their reading comprehension.

Questions and Activities to Build Background Knowledge:

1. Look at the front cover of the book and read the title. What do you think this book will be about?
2. What do you already know about this topic?
3. Take a book walk and skim the pages. Look at the table of contents, photographs, captions, and bold words. Did these text features give you any information or predictions about what you will read in this book?

Vocabulary: *Vocabulary Is Key to Reading Comprehension*

Use the following directions to prompt a conversation about each word.

- Read the vocabulary words.
- What comes to mind when you see each word?
- What do you think each word means?

Vocabulary Words:
- agriculture
- caucus
- citizenship
- colony
- discrimination
- independence
- passport
- preservation

During Reading: *Reading for Meaning and Understanding*

To achieve deep comprehension of a book, children are encouraged to use close reading strategies. During reading, it is important to have children stop and make connections. These connections result in deeper analysis and understanding of a book.

Close Reading a Text

During reading, have children stop and talk about the following:

- Any confusing parts
- Any unknown words
- Text to text, text to self, text to world connections
- The main idea in each chapter or heading

Encourage children to use context clues to determine the meaning of any unknown words. These strategies will help children learn to analyze the text more thoroughly as they read.

When you are finished reading this book, turn to the next-to-last page for **Text-Dependent Questions** and an **Extension Activity**.

TABLE OF CONTENTS

LOOKING TOWARD THE FUTURE 4

ACHIEVING US CITIZENSHIP 8

JUDGE SAUND, CONGRESSMAN 16

TIME LINE 21

GLOSSARY 22

INDEX 23

TEXT-DEPENDENT QUESTIONS 23

EXTENSION ACTIVITY 23

ABOUT THE AUTHOR
AND ILLUSTRATOR 24

LOOKING TOWARD THE FUTURE

Have you ever taken a risk?

Have you gone ahead without knowing how things would turn out?

Dalip Singh Saund took a lot of risks in his life with no idea how things would turn out.

Dalip eagerly boards the ship on his way to the United States. He grew up in the Punjab province of India, which was a British **colony** at that time. Dalip does not know what the future holds, but he looks out brightly toward the possibilities.

Dalip Singh Saund was born on September 20, 1899 to a Sikh family. Dalip's parents had no chance to go to school. They wanted to make sure Dalip got a good education. They built a one-room schoolhouse for their town. This set Dalip on a good path for school and for life. He went to college at the University of Punjab, graduating with a degree in math.

SIKHISM
Sikhism is a religion that started in the Punjab region of India in the 15th century.

Dalip loved helping his community. He supported **independence** for India. He expanded his childhood school, started two banks, and planted trees on a main road to provide shade for those who had to travel by walking. He did all of these things while waiting for his **passport** to go to the US.

ACHIEVING US CITIZENSHIP

Dalip arrived in New York through Ellis Island on September 27, 1920. His plan was to study in the US for three years. He didn't know it, but his true destiny would be in politics. His role models were great leaders including Mahatma Gandhi and Abraham Lincoln.

Dalip headed west to the University of California, Berkeley, where he studied **agriculture** and food **preservation**, and continued with math. He worked in canning factories in the summers to make money for school.

Dalip discovered strong anti-Asian hatred toward Chinese, Japanese, and Indian people like himself. He found safety and comfort by living with others from the Sikh community.

It was at this time that Dalip first started speaking publicly against British rule in India. Because of this, Dalip's family didn't want him returning home after he finished school. It wasn't safe. But **discrimination** made it hard for Dalip to find a job in the US. He decided to join other Indians who were farming in the Imperial Valley in California.

PUNJABI PIONEERS
Between 1899 to 1914, 6,800 Indians from the Punjab region of India came to the Imperial Valley. Mostly men, they farmed and fought for educational and **citizenship** rights.

Dalip continued to speak publicly about India. He gave a talk almost once a week! He brought a suit in his car to change into. He went to give his talks while the crops were being watered. He wanted to correct the false ideas people had about India and fight against anti-Indian attitudes in the US. He even wrote his first book, *My Mother India*. At one of his speaking events, he met the family of his future wife.

ANTI-SIKH VIOLENCE
Dalip's fight against anti-Sikh racism continues with the American Sikh Congressional **Caucus**. It was formed to combat anti-Sikh violence after 9/11. Many people wrongfully took revenge against Muslims after the attack on the Twin Towers because the attackers were Muslim. Many Sikh Americans were also killed or harmed because people thought they were Muslim.

Unlike white immigrants, Indian immigrants were not allowed to become citizens. This limited their opportunities. Dalip decided to fight for the right to become an American citizen.

Dalip started the Indian Association of America, which worked to change the law. Their efforts were successful when Congress passed a bill allowing Indian immigrants to become US citizens. Dalip became a citizen three and a half years later on December 16, 1949.

US CITIZENSHIP
Asians were barred from citizenship because of their race. Many fought for citizenship rights. In 1952, all Asian American immigrants could finally become citizens.

JUDGE SAUND, CONGRESSMAN

Once a citizen, Dalip ran for his first political office: county judge. He continued to face racial discrimination. A well-known man in town taunted him. He asked if Dalip would provide turbans for everyone who came to court or if people would have to get their own.

Dalip famously replied, "I don't care what a man has on the top of his head. All I'm interested in is what he's got inside." Dalip was elected and became known for his sharp mind.

Politics gave Dalip a sense of purpose. He wanted to serve people and his community. He decided to run for Congress as Judge Saund. Dalip had the support of his whole family; his wife, his children, and his children's spouses.

Together, they rang doorbells...
...held community barbecues...
...and got the community support to win the election!

Dalip overcame anti-Sikh and Indian prejudice and won 52 percent of the vote. He became the first Asian American, Indian American, and so far, the only Sikh American, elected to Congress. He championed many issues such as American Indian land rights and supporting small-scale farmers and small businesses. He was a strong supporter of the 1957 Civil Rights bill. He wrote a memoir titled *Congressman from India*.

After being reelected twice, Dalip suffered a stroke in 1962 that cost him his next election. It also ended his active involvement in politics. He died in 1973 after a second stroke. Dalip has been called "the unsung pioneer" of Asian American politics. His papers are collected at the University of California, Santa Barbara, and in the online South Asian American Digital Archive.

> There is no room in the United States of America for second-class citizenship.
> — Dalip Singh Saund

TIME LINE

1899   Dalip Singh Saund is born in Chhajjalwaddi, in the Punjab province of India, still a British colony.

1919   Dalip graduates with a mathematics degree from the University of Punjab.

1920   Dalip arrives in the US through Ellis Island on September 27.

1924   Dalip earns his PhD in mathematics from the University of California, Berkeley, where he also studied agriculture. Dalip moves to Westmorland in the Imperial Valley to farm.

1928   Dalip marries Marian Kosa, an immigrant from Czechoslovakia. They go on to have three children.

1930   Dalip's first book, *My Mother India*, is published.

1946   Dalip forms the Indian Association of America, one of several organizations trying to pass the Luce-Celler Act which would allow Indians to become US citizens.

1949   Dalip becomes a US citizen on December 16.

1952   Dalip is elected as a county judge. The McCarran Walter Act lifts the restrictions on citizenship so all Asian groups could become citizens.

1956   Dalip is elected to Congress. He is re-elected in 1958 and 1960.

1960   Dalip's second book, *Congressman from India*, is published.

1962   Dalip suffers a stroke and he loses reelection.

1973   Dalip Singh Saund dies in Hollywood, California, after a second stroke.

GLOSSARY

agriculture (AG-ri-kuhl-chur): farming or the raising of crops and animals

caucus (KAW-kus): a group of people who work together to promote a common cause

citizenship (SIT-i-suhn-ship): the condition of being a person who has full rights in a particular country

colony (KAH-luh-nee): a territory or country under the control of another country

discrimination (dis-krim-i-NAY-shuhn): unfair conduct toward others based on the group they are part of such as race, gender, religion, or age

independence (in-di-PEN-duhns): freedom or the condition of not being controlled

passport (PAS-port): an official document that verifies that you are a citizen of a certain country and allows you to travel across international borders

preservation (prez-ur-VAY-shuhn): keeping something in original or good condition

INDEX

Congress 14, 18, 19
Ellis Island 8
judge 16, 18
India 5, 6, 7, 10, 12, 19
Imperial Valley 10
Punjab 5, 6, 10
US citizenship 8, 15
Sikh 6, 10, 13, 19

TEXT-DEPENDENT QUESTIONS

1. What religion did Dalip practice?
2. What were some things Dalip did to improve his community in India?
3. Why did Dalip do so many speaking engagements and write a book on India?
4. What was Dalip the first to accomplish?
5. What is one job Dalip worked before he became a judge?

EXTENSION ACTIVITY

Imagine that you are elected to a political office in the future to serve the town or city you live in right now. What are some community needs you would like to focus on? What are some social and political issues that you would be interested in addressing?

ABOUT THE AUTHOR

Karen Su teaches Global Asian Studies at the University of Illinois Chicago to college students. Many of her college students are still surprised to learn that Asian immigrants were barred from US citizenship. And many college students have not learned about the many Asian Americans who have held political office in the US. She hopes readers will be inspired to find out more after learning about Dalip Singh Saund's story as the first Asian American to be elected to Congress.

ABOUT THE ILLUSTRATOR

Arlo Li is an illustrator originally from China and now based in the US. He enjoys creating bright, whimsical, and colorful illustrations and specializes in children's books. He seeks to tell stories through his work and uses tiny details to bring those stories to life. He loves bringing his unique artistic vision to every project he works on.

© 2024 Rourke Educational Media

All rights reserved. No part of this book may be reproduced or utilized in any form or by any means, electronic or mechanical including photocopying, recording, or by any information storage and retrieval system without permission in writing from the publisher.

www.rourkebooks.com

PHOTO CREDITS: pg 20: ©Danvis Collection / Alamy Stock Photo

Quote source: Dalip Singh Saund. *Congressman from India*, Satvic Books, Amritsar, India, 2002. p. 192.
Edited by: Hailey Scragg
Illustrations by: Arlo Li
Cover and interior layout by: J.J. Giddings

Library of Congress PCN Data

Dalip Singh Saund / Karen Su
(Leaders Like Us)
ISBN 978-1-73165-737-4 (hardcover)
ISBN 978-1-73165-724-4 (softcover)
ISBN 978-1-73165-750-3 (e-book)
ISBN 978-1-73165-763-3 (e-pub)
Library of Congress Control Number: 2023933237

Rourke Educational Media
Printed in the United States of America
01-1982311937